To

the

Sun,

Moon,

and Stars

To the Sun, Moon, and Stars

WRITTEN BY:
CARIZA OPANA

ILLUSTRATIONS BY:
ELLÉ OM

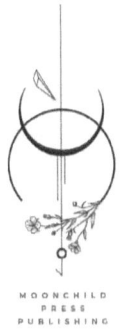

MOONCHILD
PRESS
PUBLISHING

To the Sun, Moon and Stars
Printed Edition
ISBN-13: 978-0-692-14769-6

Copyright © 2018 by Cariza Opana

Moonchild Press Publishing

This book is available at quantity discounts with bulk purchase for educational, business, or sales promotional use.

Library of Congress Control Number: 2020912824

The contents of this book are a work of fiction.
Any character resemblances to persons living or dead are purely coincidental.

All rights reserved. No part of this publication may be reproduced, stored in a retrieval system, or transmitted in any form or by any means - electronic, mechanical, photocopy, recording, or any other-except for brief quotations in printed reviews, without prior permissions of the publisher.

Foreword and Biography by: Reina Bambao www.writer-queen.com
Illustrations by: Ellé Om ellezierominoreg @ gmail.com

FOR ALL THOSE

WHO BURN

TOO BRIGHT

FOR LIFE

CONTENTS

INTRODUCTION ix

FOREWORD xi

    CHAPTER ONE 15

    TO THE SUN 17

    CHAPTER TWO 49

    TO THE MOON 50

    CHAPTER THREE 101

    TO THE STARS 103

THE ROAD TO RUIN 163

ACKNOWLEDGMENTS 176

ABOUT THE AUTHOR 179

ABOUT THE ILLUSTRATOR 180

INDEX 174

Introduction

hello friend, stranger, phantom of a face and hands who stumbled upon this collection of tiny stories,

for as long as I can remember, I had voices in my head that won't stop echoing unless I bled ink and write them on the nearest surface within grasp—table napkins, blank notebooks, my arms and wrists. I have been afraid to share these thoughts. Lately, I've realized it was one of the most terrible things I've done to myself; I've found that when you've stored them away for so long, they rot and make you feel worse in places inside of you that you never thought existed. I've finally mustered up the courage to break free and share these letters.

I hope you'll like them, I hope they'll make you feel. I hope they'll take you places and comfort you in ways I have sought comfort in other people's words. I hope they'll mean something to you. I hope they'll be something you'll remember for a really long time.

all my light and love,
 Cariza

Foreword

When I think of Cariza, I think of beauty. Beautiful photographs, beautiful words, beautiful soul making itself known behind her rare, beautiful smiles.

I was blessed in 2017 to hang out with that wellspring of loveliness practically every day for a whole month. She and I spent the summer working in various picturesque coffee shops – her revamping Paper Antlers and me getting Writer Queen off the ground – each day an outpouring of passion and creativity. On our off days, we strolled the old streets of Intramuros, read tarot cards at food parks, and walked our dogs in matching purple dresses.

It has been, so far, the most artistically satisfying time of my life.

But it wasn't all just museums and coffee and dramatic black and white outfits. That summer was also filled with long conversations about the broken homes we grew up in, the people who held our hearts wrong, and the depression that trailed behind us like an ominous Grim. There were secrets, fears, and confessions passed between us like furtive notes in class that weren't capture in our Instagram photographs.

In Cariza, I found someone who delved into her darkness and tried to understand her monsters in the best way she knew how: by wrestling them into the light, slaying them, and writing with their blood as ink on a page. I've been awed – during that summer and beyond – by her willingness to stage this battle where people can see. (Oddly enough, while it is she who is laying herself bare with her words, it is the reader, who gets a punch to the gut.)

It takes bravery to be honest with another person, to reach out to them with the broken parts of you and hope they will want to connect. I am grateful that Cariza has chosen to reach out to me, and so, so very proud that she has been brave enough to write this book to connect with you. The way she harnesses that courage is the most beautiful – and inspiring – thing yet about her.

Her words have a gift for making me feel that I am not walking this world or facing my struggles alone.

Cariza is my dear, dear friend, and I hope her book will be yours too.

Reina Bambao

PART I
TO THE SUN

I already knew you were too far for me to reach.

The First Letter

I want to promise you many things

but I can't find a way to tell them.

There are grapevines

of proses in my throat

and none of them sound right.

Until I figure out

how to punch love

out of my teeth

I'll keep them for now,

I just can't figure out

which one hits me

the most among all these bruises.

This is not the only sign

No one told me how to love someone right. Through years and years of watching romantic films and novels, I've been fed the most unrealistic ideas about how relationships should be like. Most of the time I wander around the abyss, not knowing what I'm doing. But I do know this: it shouldn't hurt this much. I shouldn't be living in constant fear of being left alone and reduced to dust. I shouldn't be full of wondering on whether or not you love me back just as much.

(WHAT THEY SAID IS

PROBABLY TRUE.)

I'm losing. I'm on the verge of putting our
love on hold for irrational fear. It feels
like the butterflies in my stomach are
long dead and they are now replaced
by a black hole, eating its way out of
my throat. My head is all shipwrecks
and doubts because all I could think
about are oceans, oceans, oceans: how
there are waves ebbing and flowing
shores hours away from you and you
aren't near.

It's not just the distance – it is us.

Tornadoes and tsunamis don't go well together. Even then I already knew you were too far for me to reach. I'm not a part of your life. I'm a guest. I'm only a guest, I'm only a guest.

> I can't stay too long,
>
> you don't need me in here.

I know that you'll love someone else
>   someday. That day will soon come: I'll
>   wake up and it'll creep out from under
>   my bed and wash over me like I've
>   always known it will.

I'll let my feet touch the floor and it'll sink in, knowing that this was the day I'll have to let you sail away into the ocean, leaving me stranded on the shore.

I'll make my morning coffee with trembling hands, realizing that I would rather have the oceans and walls, than life without you at all.

Memories

There are many things I won't forget in my life.

The lyrics of Skinny Love, how I like my coffee, the first time we met. The way you were seated on the couch, eyes fixed on the television as I walked through the door. The way I was hesitant to shake your hand at first, because yes, I've heard about you and yes, I've heard what you thought about me. You were cracked glass and fallen debris, I was a lonely prayer.

I won't forget all the times I tried to stop myself from caring too much, I won't forget the pouring rain. And I won't forget the times I fumbled my way through your path. How I kept falling and missing my steps and trying to skip all the broken glass until I decided screw it, everything feels different with you and yes, I'd like to give us a chance.

I know I once said that I would never give love a second unless I've found someone whom I could drown in forever.

Someone who is drenched in hopeful promises and sunrise, someone whom I can love so much my heart cracks and spills out everything it keeps as a secret. I said this to you as I laugh halfheartedly

I knew then I wouldn't subject myself into being in love. Yet here I am. It's as if all those moments we shared were put together deliberately by the universe, shaking its head, saying, oh dear child, must you learn this way, and of course, I had no choice.

That night when you held the steering wheel with trembling hands as I went through my thoughts, I just knew. That night when we were walking in a desolate park and you were spinning me with the music only we can hear, I just knew. That night when you cut me off mid-sentence with your lips, because there were too many words to say yet they can all be told with one kiss, and it was too late at night and I was leaving, but we couldn't let go of the night just yet –

I just knew.

The Secondhand Lover

I've told him once that I can't help

but feel like a secondhand lover,

like the self I have

whenever I walk into antique coffee shops

and garage sales.

She has explored worlds inside of him

decades before I came in,

and the first time I traced maps on his skin

it felt incomplete.

It was only after I realized
it's because
he is only left with pieces
of what she has wrecked.

But I'd take him in –
I'd always take him in.
I've learned to shape the chaos
into constellations.

Though it is not in my place to rebuild him,
I still love him,
completely and utterly,

and I hope to be there when he becomes
    whole.

Don't Make Homes Out of People

I feel like I have to etch it on my wrist, so I won't ever forget: don't make homes out of people. Yet here I am again, doing it like an old habit I can't grow out of. I love him so much my head hurts. Everything aches like stars in my veins collapse at the mere thought of what we have, and pursuing other things in life such as days in New York or leaving doesn't seem to matter.

I used to love leaving. I used to think I was
 always meant to move – and move I did,
 to every place, to everywhere. I still
 somehow feel the same, in countries I've
 been and places I frequent. Now it seems
 like the loneliness only gets worse and
 worse. I've had too many goodbyes in
 this lifetime, I think, but I am still not
 good at it.

Every goodbye feels lonelier than the last. It is
 with him, anywhere I may be in the
 world, where I feel like I am home.

You should never make homes out of people,
> they said, yet here I am.

But I love him, I love him, dear god, I love
> him so much, I'd forgotten how much I
> loved leaving.

DESIRE

You

are a tragedy of

words and lies,

of heartache and empty spaces.

Every sane thought

that haunts my head

tells me that I should run

from the man of a thousand faces.

Yet I find myself,

searching for the language

that my heart doesn't have.

So here it is, I stand fearless,

giving in to love,

giving in to hope,

giving in to silence

PART II
TO THE MOON

I used to think
we were two halves of a whole
Now, I think
we were always better off
with distance

Accidents

Here you are – always holding out for that one hope that he was wrong. That someday, someone would knock in your door and see through your cracks and decide that these things you hide within yourself doesn't matter. They won't treat you like an abandoned porcelain doll; they won't tape up your imperfections and repaint over your scars. They'd take you in as a whole. You'll realize that sometimes, people just accept. No hesitations, no questions asked.

And you'll love them, dear god, you'll really love them. You'll feel complete. You'd bring them inside the world of the broken, show them that things could be beautiful even if they are smashed into pieces. You'd fall around them thinking that there is someone out there who finally understands.

But love is not just about understanding someone completely, love doesn't quite end in acceptance. And you'll learn this, one morning, when you stretch out your arm in your sheets and all you could reach is an empty space.

You'd get up and walk around your apartment, bare feet on the cold floor and you'd find everything is the same as before –

    all cracked, broken, and empty.

.

This is when you'll finally learn that
    sometimes, whether or not we're whole,
    people just leave.

No hesitations, no questions asked.

Maybe some things aren't meant to last.

Dear Stranger,

One.

I'm going to tell you now that I'm a bit harder to love than most people. It's because I grew up with ghosts at my home and fallen debris. I turned myself into an armor of steel, so I would be protected from slashes and whips and people like you who might break me.

Two.

Sometimes I will need you to cut through my barriers and reach me. Sometimes I will need you to knock on my door when it's closed.

Sometimes I will need you to love me a little bit louder.

Three.
Dear Stranger, I'm going to tell you now that if you are here to stay, I will ask for too much.

Four.
I have a mixed-up relationship with my depression, dearest. It comes, and it goes, and sometimes it takes over and I can't control it. I will need you to hold my hair and keep my head up when I vomit my life all over the sink.

FIVE.

> I won't ask you to tell me that things are going to be okay, because I have enough wisdom to know that it won't always be. I won't ask you to hold my hand and tell me to turn over to self-love, because I don't have any.

SIX.

> Self-love is a blanket I cover myself when I go to sleep at night, occasionally punctured with holes and flaws whenever my thoughts have taken over or when someone throws hurtful words at me.

.

Self-love is a luxury I couldn't afford, not when I spent this long drowning in too much loathing.

Seven.

Dear Stranger, I am not alright. I'll be okay on some days and I will laugh at your jokes and hug you tight and kiss your lips. I'll believe in a parallel world where my life isn't taken over by a lonely sky. I'll fumble my way through crossroads and horizons, just so I could meet you halfway. I won't leave you alone and I'll try harder to get to you, it'll just take time for me to get there day by day.

I will ask for you to be extra patient with me
    and careful, as I don't know what I'm
    doing.

Eight.

I kept all the butterflies in my stomach in a jar
    hidden somewhere in my closet. I would
    need them at nights when I'm tangled up
    in your sheets and I need to feel
    something.

Nine.

This would be a burden, but I would ask you
    to keep me away from my family.

Ten.

Dear Stranger, for all of this,
    I am sorry.
I just need you to love me.

THIS IS ALL YOU HAVE TO KNOW

You once said you'd never let yourself fall for me and I almost believed you. I've met strangers on sidewalks and they were more familiar to me than your footsteps at my door. I've drowned love letters in whiskeys and they all remain unsent, burned down my lungs as I tried to forget. I swear there was a time I could almost smell you in my sheets. How it once felt like you were the lingering smoke in my cup of coffee.

The nights turned in and they weren't as quiet as they used to be. In my heart they thundered and roared and poured ashes of rain, convincing myself that the only way I could ever get over you was to tell you that at least I tried. Yet I read thirty poems today, and they all reminded me of you. I can't shake the nagging thought that surely you must have a reason, you always have a reason. But my insides feel like they're tying themselves into knots and I'm all missing pieces.

My heart feels like a flower plucked off from a garden before it even had the chance to bloom.

So maybe one day I'll be standing in the front porch of my own home, taking in the morning breeze. I'll be kissing my husband goodbye and good luck for work on the cheek and I'll remember the way we used to be.

How we loved, and it was beautiful and how we burned through the break and fall.

How unfair it was that despite that, we couldn't make it
　　　　　after all.

What a Waste

You once said

you'd grab a piece of the sky

and turn it into time

to wait for me,

but I said

I didn't want it.

Because someday,

when I still couldn't love you

in the way you needed to be,

you'll ask for your hourglass back.

And I can't

give you

spilled sand

I can't hold

in my hands.

Sometimes Letting Go Isn't a Terrible Thing

ONE.

They were wrong when they said some things last forever if you decide to keep them. I think the world tells you this to steer you away from the haunting truth that nothing lasts that long. People come and go like seasons in your life. Even your favorite milk has an expiration date. All things that begin will eventually have an end.

TWO.

This destruction was inevitable.

THREE.

Some people would make homes out of you and take advantage of your welcome mat. They would drink all your wine and sleep on your couch and make you feel you're important, and then leave you out of the blue with nothing to drink and nowhere to sleep. Some would need you too much.

Dearest, you'd have to break away. These people would drown you out in the ocean and leave you washed up off shore. You'd soon feel empty, so drained out, because once again, you have given too much.

FOUR.

There are those who would feel like you're the missing puzzle piece in their life mystery. Take a deep breath and remind yourself, people are not made up of broken halves and the universe did not place you in here to complete these people. You are the sun, and you should not need to burn yourself out just to make others feel whole.

FIVE.

Someday when you realize the world isn't made of cottage cheese and confetti, and people who won't always be there for you, you'll learn how to let them go like unwanted strands under the sink.

SIX.

And for those who have shook themselves
    all over your welcome mat and left
    bread crumbs on your floor, they'd find
    another home.

As for you, your walls are grapevines and
    thunderstorms, and this time, you are
    better.

STITCHES

In the world of dreams
was where we met,
we clung unto a fragile thread
and lay underneath
a blanket of stars.
We drowned echoes in the wind,
and waited for the sun
to pick us apart.

In the world of love,
we met again.
We handed each other
keys to our own worlds,
and got drunk enough
to let
the skies swallow us whole.

In the world of brokenness,

was where we said goodbye.

We stitched our shadows together,

and planted flowers

in our souls,

thinking the stars

won't stand a chance

if we treated them like fools.

In the world of hope,

I thought I'd see him here.

But it's been too long, I think

and I plucked out

these petals

until they all disappeared.

'Come and find me,

    when these flowers start to grow.'

Maybe

in the world of scars,

I can unstitch our shadows apart.

And when we find each other,

I'll have the strength

to finally rip out

the flowers in his heart.

.

I CAN'T HOLD YOU WELL LIKE YOUR SECRETS

Back then before I go to sleep,
> I'd befriend the shadows on my walls
>
> and ignore how much I'm haunted
>
> by your face in fragments.

There used to be days that
> just walk through me,
>
> and I can't hold them well
>
> enough like your secrets.

I thought I will never get past
> how much the world has gotten too
>
> heavy for
>
> my shoulders to bear.

If life were a game of
    unrequited loneliness,
    I'd be winning out of despair.
I hoped when I look back
    at the years I spent with you,
I'll no longer feel much longing.
I just wished when
    we were at the downfall,
I have foreseen the ending.
But now when I look at the horizon, they
    no longer scream your name.
And when the sun seeps through
    my curtains each morning,
I take comfort in knowing
    I'm no longer playing this game.

COFFEE STAINS

I was the coffee and you were wine,
I wanted to stain your favorite white
    shirt and wreck it,
    the way you got me too drunk
    to count constellations in my sleep.
I want your silhouette to stop
    burning through the back of my eyelids,
    for these echoes taking over my head
    to stop sounding like voices
    screaming at me
    every 3am.
Lately, sunsets have been looking at
    me with sad eyes;
    they seem to tell me
I've seen enough of them in a lifetime.

Maybe someday, I will stop you from
> passing through my lips like a ghost,
> how often your name
> seems to find its way
> in between these short, hollow breaths.

I don't need you anymore,
> at least
> > not in the way the horizon breaks
> > and makes way for the sun
> > to give meaning to another day.

Back then, I thought
> they should have songs
> written about you
> but now, not really.

You deserve broken proses,
> and bitter coffee.

Ghost Lines

I guess I like to get lost
 in all these made up conversations.

PART III
TO THE STARS

I'm a mess of contradictions
and you're the unlucky one
who is caught up in the crossfire.

What If

It was dark, and it was raining and if it were a different circumstance in a possible different universe, you would've hated it. But you were in this one – the realest one – and you both were laughing and running and for a split second, nothing else mattered. You think to yourself, if you could spend the rest of your life just laughing like this, raindrops kissing your cheeks, not caring about the inevitable morning that lies ahead, and the next ones after that, then it wouldn't be so bad at all. The whole world seems so much brighter despite the rain.

But even though her smile reminds you of the way flowers turn to the sun in spring and she smells like frail hope and a splash of promise, even though she is here, and she is laughing, and she is real – it's quite funny how close someone could be to you and yet there is so much distance. You can feel it, as the skies cried, and the wind gets harsher, that she would someday pull away. So, when she looks at you, millions of words unsaid, hanging above you both in a trail of what if's, it all shatters down and falls around you with the pouring rain.

Because there was no other reality that existed besides this – you love her, but she belonged to someone else. And when she hugs you her last goodbye, you wished, in that second, that there could be thousands of other moments just like this. You wished time would stop, like it would've happened in movies, just so you could hold on to this – to her – just a bit longer. But reality only lets you have two seconds at most, and it was completely unfair, and when she walks away you stand there, frozen, helplessly staring at the empty space that stretches farther and farther between you and her.

There was nothing else, but the rain.

The Art of Burning Bridges

ONE.

I told myself I shouldn't write about you yet here I am, mounting the footsteps and flinging myself off the cliffs of come what may, because sometimes the world gets too much, and I need a space to breathe in.

TWO.

I used to think we were two halves of a whole.

> Now, I think we were always better off with distance.

THREE.

> The reality is I cannot save you. And I can't keep fooling myself into thinking that I can; you love your tragedies so much you always choose to drown in them, and I will always try to reach out and keep you from drowning even though I you'd rather stay in there.

FOUR.

Sometimes the ones we love cannot break us free from the chains that bind us, sometimes we're the ones who lock them up.

FIVE.

I've had enough.

SIX.

I will stop singing to your symphony of one tragedy after another. I will stop pulling out the weeds wherever you keep planting them. If I keep this up I will be overrun with you, and I choose to never have to deal with all of this again.

SEVEN.

Sometimes, the ones we want to love will leave us when we get too much. Sometimes, we're the only ones left.

EIGHT.

It took me a while to realize that our music doesn't always go well together.

NINE.

I need to save myself too.

YOUR LOVE IS NOT A PILL AND IT CAN'T HEAL ME

I can't handle all these mixed signals and uneven signs. I'd much rather get past the charade and skip the race, as we're getting too old for these games. I'm a mess of contradictions and you're the unlucky one who is caught up in the crossfire. I'm not sure if I can be with you in the ways you needed to be loved.

My father used to warn me about people made out of hurricanes

One day, I'll leave you and you'll hate me. You'll hate me so much I won't be able to breathe from the clouds you'd rip from the skies out of despair. I will hate myself even more for trying to drown in you, while knowing at the same time we couldn't work. This is a sin I'm not prepared to make.

It's unfair for you to make me need you while you're still befriending the shadows she left on your walls I know at the back of my mind how much I need you, how there are parts of me that ache and are desolate when you're not there. You are the words I can't seem to write and stash away in those paper napkins when I take afternoons off coffee houses, the butterflies I've caged in my stomach, so I won't have to feel them after all those somersaults. If there is music in my head I would write songs after you.

And I would tune into them and make the most out of the rhythm, because back then I thought we went well together as harmoniously as a symphony. But you don't need me in the way that I am constantly needing you. You remind me of the reason why I purposely set up walls and shut people off, because I have been through these games before and now I don't want to play. Yet you dragged me into the court with you and left me just as I was learning the rules of your game.

THE REALITY OF IT ALL

I want to be there for you and I want to love you in ways that she has never had, but at the same time I don't want to give parts of myself to make you whole. I can't keep creating homes out of people and expecting they'd cherish my presence back with a welcome mat. I've learned countless times that is not how the world works. It is my fault, it is my fault, really, for setting you up so high and letting myself get the best out of my expectations. The idiocy of it all baffles me and I can't believe I let myself get into this kind of situation.

I THOUGHT I'VE ALREADY LEARNED HOW TO CUT OFF BRIDGES

It feels like walking on broken glass, the way I tiptoe myself around you. I am slowly cautious of my actions, not knowing whether or not you're getting the right messages. I had to constantly remind myself to never let you cross that bridge to me, for there is so much room for you in here. These nights are already made of me counting down the hours until you come to me in hidden spaces.

One day I would stop being chased by your ghost and the way you almost got to me.

Sometimes I Define People by the Way They Take Their Coffee

Some people you meet are puzzles waiting to be finished, some of them are games you'd never want to play. And some of them are echoes of your past you don't want to be reminded of. Then there are some people who are too broken to love and to be loved in return, and I thought I was one of those people. When you told me your story over those morning walks I wish it never happened, because you let me in so easily. I should've seen that as a barrier, not as an open door.

Truthfully, I am not as guarded as I try to be. I tell the world that my walls are made of grapevines and thunderstorms, but I crumble at the slightest hint of affection.

Eleven Steps on How to Not Need Somebody

One.

I wish I were the kind of person that people would remember after meeting for the first time. But no, I am often easily dismissed. If people were places I am a sidewalk, you'll never pass by; the alleys are too dark, the steps are too narrow, and it is not worth your time.

Two.

Some people write songs for moments like this. I write endless proses. In my head, there were a million things left unsaid and I wanted to break free of them, but I was a dark alley and you were those colored lights, and I hold too many secrets to spill them all to you after a handful of conversations.

Three.

Lately, I've been trying to find the right words to string together and form a harmony that could be meaningful, but I have yet to find the notes that would describe this chaos perfectly.

FOUR.

I don't want to let you get to me in all these hidden spaces I didn't even know existed, only for you to become a poem that I can never write. The more you try to get to me the more I'll stay further away until someday I'll be Alaska, and the miles between us will be more than from here to Russia.

FIVE.

I know that I could love you in ways no one has ever had, but at the same time I don't want to give you parts of myself just to make you whole.

SIX.

The more I try to stop the more I am dooming myself to feel, I think. My days seem incomplete without your words to soothe me and assure me of things I don't even know about myself. I've been lonely for too long.

SEVEN.

Every time you get to me I could feel myself crack open and tip my hourglass over the cliff. But I can't be like this and it frightens me.

EIGHT.

I am terrified I would end up needing you, and I've already clung on to a lot of almosts.

NINE.

If this is different, I can only hope you'd prove me wrong.

(And I really hope you'd prove me wrong, as I have been lonely for too long).

TEN.

If I could give you a twisted sunset I would, just so when you look at shades of orange and blue, you'd be reminded of me.

I'm going to push you further away now, and you can come to me when you're ready.

ELEVEN.

I don't know how to end this.

Once upon a time

I had friends. I had someone who would make up scenarios in her head, just to see if someone cares enough to listen. It is through her where I learned that friendships aren't forever and some people, are merely passersby in your life and none of them are meant to stay. It is quite a pity, since I turned my heart into her home and in the end, she wanted none of what I had to offer.

ONCE UPON A TIME

people around me were falling apart. Some hearts that were stored for too long in cages were finally set free. Others threw away their keys. I only had to watch and wait patiently for the skies to swallow me. I thought I would fly, that I would be saved.

I didn't. I wasn't.

ONCE UPON A TIME

there was a girl filled with passion and fire, and every so often, she would burn her way through my lungs and tie together words in a way that would touch others. She would sit by herself and be comforted by her own presence, her own silence. She was at still with happiness.

The longer she lived, the more she died.

Once upon a time

I wrote a letter and stashed it inside a bottle and threw it away into the sea. I watched it become smaller and smaller speck of dust as the ocean tried to swallow it with each roaring wave. I watched it disappear into the horizon and I hoped it would never come back to me untouched. Until now, I'm hoping for someone to read it and understand.

I never got a reply.

.

Horoscope

ARIES

I know lately your heart has been stretching out the distance, that the world seems so much bigger when measured in miles and time zones. But eventually you'll meet them halfway, you'll find them in your own hiding place. Hold on to that hope and don't let go.

TAURUS

You are an earthquake that sends ripples in the water and cracks on the ground.

You are many, many beautiful things. Don't let those voices trample upon your worth.

GEMINI

Someone once said that there are cracks in everything so light could come in. Your cracks aren't imperfections, they're the ones that keep you whole.

CANCER

It's time to stop praying to the skies and wishing they'd go back to you, dearest. If you try and look closely, the world is bigger than the patch of rain cloud you keep praying unto.

LEO

Your heart is so big it could cover the borders of Alaska, however don't open it often as a home to people who are only meant to come in your life as guests. When things don't go well some of them would move on to their next destinations as if it were nothing, as if you were only meant to be a temporary shelter. Your home is meant for the ones who will stay, through thunderstorms and rain.

VIRGO

Don't be afraid to create beautiful things. The world could never have enough color and glitter. If you look at your hands and you see roadmaps and ink splatters, be proud of how much you've done.

LIBRA

Dearest, you are not a puzzle piece whose sole purpose in the world is to complete others.

SCORPIO

We all tend to burn things whether or not on purpose: candlesticks, toast, or bridges. Don't hate yourself for being made of passion and fire. One day you'd meet someone who'd burn with you just as much, without leaving scorch marks on your heart.

SAGITTARIUS

Love is not meant to hurt you so much you'd bleed. It is meant as a sigh of relief, a pair of arms you can curl yourself up into and say, "I'm so glad to be home."

You deserve someone to go home to, child.

Don't let anyone tell you otherwise.

CAPRICORN

There are many different ways that people could wear bravery. Some of them were armors, some of them wear masks. I've always admired the way you wear your heart on your sleeves.

AQUARIUS

Kindness does not equate to weakness, no matter what people say. Always be kind, even if the world is lashing out on you with sharp tongues. Always be kind, even if they tell you that in doing so, your heart will be burdened.

PISCES

Life is only as beautiful as you make it out to be, so open up your curtains and wipe your cheeks. Joy could be found even in the littlest things, like your favorite cup of coffee or warm sweater sleeves.

Epilogue

The Road to Ruin

There was once a girl who never really thought much about love. When she thinks of it, she is reminded of the Fitzgeralds and the days when their marriage was once without a trace of destruction. She thinks of stories about defying all odds once two people are together. Love existed in fantasies and books, in dreams that hung through clouds and were out of reach. It most definitely didn't exist in the world she lives in.

I wish I could write that she met a boy who knocked her off her high pedestal and made her fall madly, but alas, this story, the one I'm about to tell you, is not that easy. The girl had to travel and wander through various cities, searching for answers, and the boy had to take long, midnight drives to the outskirts of town before they will find each other. And in many more days after that, somewhere in the nights that would consist of spontaneous midnight coffee runs, passenger seat concerts, and an endless exchange of stories and random photographs, they will fall in love.

Much later, neither won't be able to tell you the exact moment it happened.

I should warn beforehand that this is not a love story. I wish I could tell it like it was but sadly, love stories are peppered with grandeur displays of heroic affection, telling us that all forces in the world could never compete against two people who have feelings for each other. This story is far from that. It is far from perfect too, because real stories aren't always perfectly polished and edited and told in the right sequence like the ones published on paper.

In reality, there are different forces in the world that could either bring two people together or rip them apart. The universe likes to play games, you see. Some people lose each other, because not all of us were born to fight. If you've been slashed with scars for so long, at one point you'll admit defeat. Some people would battle their ways through these armies, despite having been knocked down again and again. They will shout into the universe that they'll do whatever it takes to win. Some people are lucky enough to never have wars they need to face. Some people don't survive them at all.

Many different forces, many different games.

Some people stay, some people leave.

This story started years ago, long before they met. They were living different lives, embarking on separate roads, completely immersed in their own worlds without knowing the other person existed. He dated someone and gave his all; they taught each other the blissful rush of being with someone, the bright specks of happiness that come from moments shared. They went on road trips and had dinner dates and were happy for a time. Yet one day, she woke up, counted ghost stars in the sky and told him,

"I'm letting you go."

One of the forces in the world that some of us face are people made out of hurricanes, sent by the gods who are jealous of a petty thing such as mortal love, and they'll leave piles and piles of destruction in their wake.

The worst ones are the ones who don't say goodbye.

The boy drowned himself in cheap beer and wine. He drove recklessly in the rain. He laid in bed for hours without moving an inch, wishing for the blankets to swallow him whole. He wasted half a year looking for second chances.

It was a Friday evening when *he*, on the verge of mending broken pieces of himself, seated on the edge of a leather couch waiting for a miracle, would meet *her*, standing below the ceiling lights, treading on her path like wisps of dandelions blown in the wind, praying for an ending.

They didn't like each other at first, no. There were no harmonious symphonies at the first time they shook hands. That happened much later. It took knocking down walls, card games that lasted all night and morning walks in search of coffee in the middle of a deserted island before they reached a mutual understanding of each other.

"I've never met anyone like him before." She confided in her friend.

Of course, he is kind and sweet and a Sunday morning comfort she didn't know she needed, but she didn't know this at the time.

Among the forces that wreck, there is another that is neither hurricane nor thunderstorm, and unlike friendships that end. These are people who wished to love and be loved in return. They are not sinners and they don't have wrong intentions. However, their love is often misplaced, and they're left burdened in the sky before they go in another pursuit of someone new.

There was another boy.

He was gentle, he was sweet, and he was full of promises he wished to keep. He was whole, this one; he didn't have any broken parts he needed to mend, he didn't have the need to shield himself. He was bold and assuring and from the very beginning, he was clear of his intentions. But there were still many things he didn't understand.

"Do you like him?" the broken boy teasingly asked once. It was a weekend. He was free, and he needed someone to hang out with. She was the first person he asked.

"We hang out sometimes," she replied.

"Oh," was all he said.

The world loves to play games and every so often, they are cruel enough to make you feel like pawns on a chess board. It's not fun to feel vulnerable and scared and to lie bare in front of the one you love with so much uncertainty you could feel yourself snap in half. There were no rules in this game, but someone always has to lose.

The broken boy would take escape drives to clear his head, would often wonder if, in the end, there was a kind force in the universe that will make one huge difference. He wandered through the realm of possibilities about her choosing the other boy who wasn't broken, who was bold, who was sure. He wondered, most of all, if he was ready to love again.

(The other boy, on the other hand, would always put his effort in the wrong place.)

Still, she took him to watch plays, taught him how she orders her coffee. She told him stories about work, about how she longed for a great escape from monotonous days that would take her far away and closer to her dreams. They had conversations that spiral from warped realities she has conjured in her mind to an existential crisis about life, from ambitions and family problems to funny articles found online. They laughed over the silliest things, the craziest things. They would leave together late in the evening, in search of cupcakes to satisfy sudden cravings, of the best cup of coffee in the city.

In a way, he knew he'd have to hide how he felt. He tried his best to stay away. His feelings have no place wherein the other boy exists and would only break a girl who didn't believe in love. But there are other forces that were much, much worse than that.

It was November. He found out she was leaving.

"Do you know when?" he asked her one night, his heart thumping so loudly if she listened carefully through the barriers of silence, she could've heard them.

"I don't know, but it's probably next year."

"Okay."

Out of the many forces the universe would throw in to keep two people apart, people made out of hurricanes, words that would leave you shattered into a thousand glass shards, missed risks and opportunities, people with love and affections misplaced, the biggest and worst culprit of them all was distance.

It was a cold, night without any stars. She was with the whole one, in a desolate parking lot, thousands of words that were wishing to be said loom over them with the blank sky when he asked,

"Do you love him?"

Surely, at some point, he must've known. There were always those small moments of ultimatum, moments when she's left in wonder on whom she could turn to and trust. And it was always him, the broken one, the one who also knows what the road to ruin feels like. It wasn't this boy, with bold gifts and intentions misplaced. It was him, the broken boy, who can laugh with her as she sings her way half-key through a Spotify playlist; the broken boy, whom she can tell childhood stories of sleepy singing angels on stage; the broken boy, who knows her deepest fears without asking. Who knew, that in the months she'd spent running away from the one thing she refuses to believe the most, she'd fallen in love without even knowing it.

In another story, she could've loved this other boy if she tried.

But that is not a story I wish to tell.

"I'm letting you go," she said. Whoever said it was easy to tell someone you cannot love them in the way they needed to be? "I'm sorry."

After all, there are some people who know how to say goodbye.

(But they still hurt, each and every single time.)

Here's a little secret no one tells you about life. In novels and movies wherein, you see two people defying so many odds to stay together, it happens in this world too. It's just that these wars don't come in the form of dragons you have to slay to get to the castle and win the girl. Some of these wars come in the smallest bits of reality, most of them are forces of the universe we have to face.

In this story, there wasn't a dragon standing in the way. Only a couple of words written on cards.

They were on their way home. It was quiet, there was a long drive ahead of them and fear hung in the air. This time, she was sure.

"I have something to tell you," she said, rifling through her purse and taking out cards with words sometimes visible in the passing streetlights.

Before I go any further, let me tell you that this story has no end. To tell you the truth, I have no slightest idea on how I should end it. There were more things that happened after that night, such as walk-dancing through the sidewalk past midnight, twirling in music no one else can hear, playing hide and seek in an empty park, exchanging silliest photos when we were kids. I told you this wasn't a love story. However, it's a story about treacherous roads that led two people to fall in love with each other. About big fights regarding the impending future and the haunting past, about two people risking everything without knowing what is going to happen next. About nights that are made of planning, wishing, waiting. About kisses that are sent through a flood wave of messages. About losing habits, adjusting to situations when the other wasn't there. About waking up alone in bed, in a different time zone, on the other side of the world. About two people still trying to make it work against the biggest and worst force the universe had to throw in existence.

He cut her off mid-sentence with trembling lips, and suddenly, everything made sense.

There is a Chinese myth called, "the red string of fate." It is said that two people, despite time, circumstance, or any force the world could muster, simply belong together. This string may be forgotten in different paths crossed, tangled in out of place timing through various situations, and stretched beyond 5,000 miles worth of distance. Later on, I learned that love wasn't epic and it won't save you from dragons, evil antagonists set on destroying peace, and all the forces in the world. Love is a red string connecting two people – it isn't perfect, it isn't smooth sailing. It is, however, a force that is bigger than two people deciding to face these battles together. It is learning how to hold someone's secrets like 2 am, knowing how someone likes to take their coffee. It is midnight drives to nowhere, dancing without music on the sidewalk. It is fighting about things in the past that shouldn't be said, it is conversations that could go on forever. It is understanding someone and taking them at their best and at their worst, without hesitation. It is drinking cheap wine that tastes awful, it is many failed attempts at surprises. It is kissing him for the first time and knowing he is the only person you want to kiss for the rest of your life. It is moments that change you, that make you go from one hopeless cynic to one firm believer. And in that night, in a sanctuary inside a small red car, despite the looming gloom that was to happen in a few weeks, I knew I'd always choose him, every time. In many different lifetimes. In all the universes that exist. Because this was the kind of love that I now believed in.

He cried the night before I left.

"I don't know what's going to happen to us," he said.

"Neither do I," I replied.

I told you that goodbyes hurt every time.

But thankfully, this one wasn't the last.

INDEX

<u>CONTENTS</u>	vi
<u>INTRODUCTION</u>	ix
<u>FOREWORD</u>	xi
<u>PART I – TO THE SUN</u>	15
THE FIRST LETTER	19
THIS IS NOT THE ONLY SIGN	21
MEMORIES	29
THE SECONDHAND LOVER	37
DON'T MAKE HOMES OUT OF PEOPLE	41
DESIRE	47
<u>PART II – TO THE MOON</u>	49
ACCIDENTS	53
DEAR STRANGER	59
THIS IS ALL YOU HAVE TO KNOW	69
WHAT A WASTE	75
SOMETIMES LETTING GO ISN'T A TERRIBLE THING	77

STITCHES	85
I CAN'T HOLD YOU WELL LIKE YOUR SECRETS	91
COFFEE STAINS	95
GHOST LINES	99

PART III – TO THE STARS	101

WHAT IF	105
THE ART OF BURNING BRIDGES	111
YOUR LOVE IS NOT A PILL AND IT CAN'T HEAL ME	119
MY FATHER USED TO WARN ME ABOUT PEOPLE MADE OUT OF HURRICANES	119
THE REALITY OF IT ALL	125
I THOUGHT I'VE ALREADY LEARNED TO CUT OFF BRIDGES	127
SOMETIMES I DEFINE PEOPLE BY THE WAY THEY TAKE THEIR COFFEE	129
ELEVEN STEPS ON HOW NOT TO NEED SOMEBODY	133
ONCE UPON A TIME	143
HOROSCOPE	149

EPILOGUE – THE ROAD TO RUIN	163

Acknowledgments

In the beginning stages of this book, it was just me, my thoughts, and a pen. Nothing would have been possible without these people.

To my editor, my best friend, Reina Bambao. Thank you for being the kindest, most understanding person.

To my soulmate, Pia, who I share many of my dreams with.

To my friends, Jessa, Christine, Iris, Sarah. Thank you for bringing light into my life.

To the ones who frequent Paper Antlers. Thank you for your unwavering encouragement and support that push me to continue writing. Thank you for inspiring me endlessly.

To my siblings who inspire so much laughter and joy.

To my beautiful mom who is the strongest person that I know. Thank you for sharing your love of language with me.

To Jaime, who never gets tired of my letters, who I will always love more than all the words I can possibly string together. You keep telling me that between the two of us, I'm the one with words, but you're always the one who knows exactly what to say at the right moments. Thank you for making me shine, for believing in me and in my dreams. I wouldn't have done it all without your words.

And to you, because you've decided that this collection of mine is worth having in your hands. Thank you for welcoming my stories in your life.

About the Author

Cariza hopes her words are able to inspire, bring comfort, and take people to different places. Her works have been published in various platforms and zines, including Thought Catalog, Eternal Remedy, Z Anthology, and Inflection.

She calls both Washington DC and Manila home and is mother to two dogs, Pancakes and Waffles, who live halfway around the world from each other.

To the Sun, Moon, and Stars is her first book.

See more of the world through Cariza's eyes at:
facebook, twitter, instagram
@PAPERANTLERS

About the Illustrator

Ellé Om is a freelance illustrator who loves to cook spaghetti. She currently lives with her husband and two cats in the Philippines.

When she is not drawing and painting, she tends to her cactus garden.

Her artworks are whimsical enough to send her audience into a dreamlike state, giving people a feeling of melancholy and nostalgia in vivid forms.

Contact her at ellezierominoreg @ gmail.com

www.ingramcontent.com/pod-product-compliance
Lightning Source LLC
Chambersburg PA
CBHW032039290426
44110CB00012B/866